WHAT'S THE DIFFERENCE?

To JC: Unmistakable, irreplaceable!

—EMMA STRACK

For my dear mother, who gave me the idea for this book.

—GUILLAUME PLANTEVIN

First published in the United States of America in 2018 by Chronicle Books LLC.

Originally published in France in 2015 under the title *Chouette ou Hibou?*
by Gallimard Jeunesse, 5, rue Gaston-Gallimard, 75007 Paris, France.

Library of Congress Cataloging-in-Publication Data Available.

ISBN 978-1-4521-6101-3

Manufactured in China.

Original French edition art direction by Élisabeth Cohat.
Original French edition design by Fleur Lauga.
Original French edition cover design by Anaïs Lemercier.
Chronicle Books cover design by Alice Seiler.
English translation by Kate Willsky.
The illustrations in this book were rendered digitally.

10 9 8 7 6 5 4 3 2

Chronicle Books LLC
680 Second Street
San Francisco, California 94107

Chronicle Books—we see things differently.
Become part of our community at www.chroniclekids.com.

WHAT'S THE DIFFERENCE?

40+ PAIRS OF THE SEEMINGLY SIMILAR

By **Emma Strack**
Illustrations by **Guillaume Plantevin**

chronicle books · san francisco

CONTENTS

ANIMALS

Viper or garter snake? Both of these cold-blooded serpents are scaly and slither, but which one has a dangerous bite?

VIPER

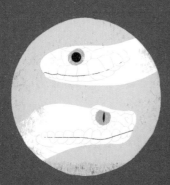

Look into my eyes . . . A garter snake has round **pupils**. Vipers' pupils are vertical slits, similar to those of a cat.

A snake's **venom glands** are only dangerous if the venom is injected. This is usually the case with the viper, which uses the very large fangs at the front of its jaw to paralyze prey.

Some garter snakes are venomous, but their bites aren't dangerous, either because they don't have **fangs**, or because their fangs are at the very back of the throat.

	VIPER	GARTER SNAKE
CLASS	• Reptilia	• Reptilia
FAMILY	• Viperidae	• Colubridae
WORLDWIDE DISTRIBUTION	• More than 200 species, including the adder, the asp, and pit vipers (like the rattlesnake, cottonmouth, and copperhead)	• At least 35 species
DISTINGUISHING FEATURES	• Vertical-slit pupils, short tail, triangular head, and fangs at the front of the jaw	• Round pupils, long tail, oval head, and fangs at the back of the throat
DANGEROUS TO HUMANS?	• Venomous	• Nonvenomous for humans
ATTACK STYLE	• Bites first to inject venom, then eats	• Bites and eats immediately
LIFESPAN	• Approximately 10 to 15 years	• 2 years

GARTER SNAKE

The garter snake is a good **swimmer**: it doesn't hesitate to stretch out on the riverbank or explore underwater. The viper often keeps its head above water while swimming.

Vipers are feared for their bite, but they're also helpful—they get rid of **unwanted rodents**!

The longest snake in the world is a **nonvenomous reticulated python**, clocking in at over 25 feet (7.6 metres).

It is night, and all is calm. Parents, children, and dogs are asleep, but outside, there's a cry: *Hoot! Hoot!* Birds of the night, the owl and the horned owl seize this quiet time to stalk their prey. These birds may look alike, but they *do* have differences—pay close attention to their plumes!

OWL

Consisting of a mass of flexible feathers, a **crest**—or **aigrette**—is a tuft on the head of certain birds, including the horned owl, some herons, and the egret.

These birds of prey vary in size: from 5 to 28 inches (12 to 70 centimetres) long, with weight ranging from less than 1.4 ounces (40 grams) for small owls to over 5.5 pounds (2.5 kilograms) for the great horned owl (*Bubo virginianus*).

There are about **50 species** of horned owls. The horned, earlike feather crests on their heads are called **plumicorns**.

	OWL	HORNED OWL
CLASS	• Aves	• Aves
ORDER	• Strigiformes	• Strigiformes
DIET	• Insects, birds, small mammals, and reptiles	• Insects, birds, and small mammals
SIZE	• 5 to 28 inches (12 to 70 centimetres)	• 5 to 28 inches (12 to 70 centimetres)
DISTINGUISHING FEATURES	• May or may not have feather crests	• Feather crests
LIFESPAN	• 4 to 30 years	• Up to 30 years

HORNED OWL

The plumage of both types of owls allows them to blend into the landscape. It also allows for completely silent flight!

These birds don't often make nests, and generally prefer to settle inside the **hollows** of trees and rocks. One species of owl (the burrowing owl) digs burrows.

All owls swallow their prey whole. The parts that they can't digest, like hair, claws, or bones, are regurgitated as **pellets**.

It's hot outside. In the garden, bees, and butterflies fly from flower to flower gathering pollen and nectar. Everything is calm when, suddenly, a jumping, energetic insect suddenly emerges from the grass. Is it a grasshopper or a cricket?

GRASSHOPPER

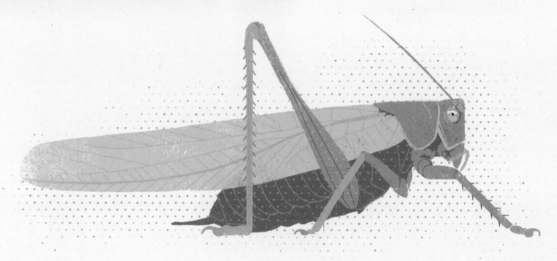

A **grasshopper**'s antennae are shorter than its body, while the antennae of a **cricket** can be longer than its body.

While grasshoppers **feed** on grasses and other plants, crickets eat plants and even meat.

Grasshoppers that you generally see are **green** and crickets are **brown**. But there are also brown grasshoppers and green crickets.

	GRASSHOPPER	CRICKET
CLASS	• Insecta	• Insecta
HABITAT	• On the ground, among the vegetation, especially dry areas with lots of grass	• On the ground, among the vegetation, especially humid areas with lots of plants
DIET	• Plants	• Plants and insects
SIZE	• 0.4 to 2.75 inches (1 to 7 centimetres) long	• 0.1 to 2 inches (0.3 to 5 centimetres) long
DISTINGUISHING FEATURES	• Able to fly; antennae are shorter than body	• Able to fly, active at night; antennae are longer than body
COLOR	• Usually green	• Usually brown
LIFESPAN	• Up to several years	• 1 year or more

CRICKET

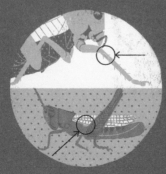

Both insects make sounds through **stridulation**. Crickets do this by rubbing their front wings together, while grasshoppers sing by rubbing their hind legs against their abdomen or front wings.

In some crickets, the **eardrum** is located on the shin of the front leg. The grasshopper's hearing organ is on its stomach.

You can recognize a female cricket by her long **ovipositor**, an organ that allows her to lay and bury her eggs. Female grasshoppers do not have distinct ovipositors, but are larger than males.

Two big ears, soft fur, and long hind legs for jumping—hares and rabbits are cousins. But how do you tell them apart?

RABBIT

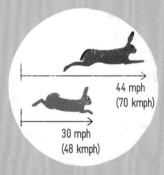

Thicker fur, longer ears, and stronger hind legs differentiate hares from wild rabbits. The ends of a hare's ears are always black, even if it has a completely white coat.

The rabbit is usually smaller than the hare, with shorter hind legs. Its **speed** is estimated to be 30 miles per hour (48 kilometres per hour), versus 44 miles per hour (70 kilometres per hour) for the hare.

The rabbit digs **burrows** and lives in colonies. The hare is a solitary animal that lives in a **nest** (a small depression in the ground) or in the grass, without digging a burrow.

Although they are **vegetarians**, hares and rabbits don't just eat carrots! They also enjoy dandelions, grains, wild grass, fruits, and herbs.

	RABBIT	**HARE**
CLASS	• Mammalia	• Mammalia
DISTRIBUTION	• Western Europe and Northern Africa	• Asia
DIET	• Leafy greens, root vegetables, fruit, wild grass, and hay	• Wild grass, dandelions, clover, roots, and seeds
SIZE	• 8 to 20 inches (20 to 50 centimetres) long	• 16 to 28 inches (40 to 70 centimetres) long
DISTINGUISHING FEATURES	• Nearly 360° peripheral vision; shorter hind legs; slower; lives in a burrow	• Nearly 360° peripheral vision; longer hind legs; faster; lives in a nest
COLOR	• Brown or gray (wild); bi- or tricolor (domesticated)	• Gray-brown and red, even white in cold regions
STATE	• Wild or domesticated	• Wild
LIFESPAN	• Approximately 3 years	• Approximately 5 years

HARE

To properly digest their food, hares and rabbits eat their own **excrement** (cecotropes) after the first digestion cycle, so that they absorb the proteins and vitamins.

The **teeth** of rabbits, hares, and all rodents project outward. Some say this is to accommodate the scratching of the grass while chewing.

A camel has two humps, as many as there are syllables in its name. And since you'll never see a camel with four humps, a dro-me-dar-y just has one!

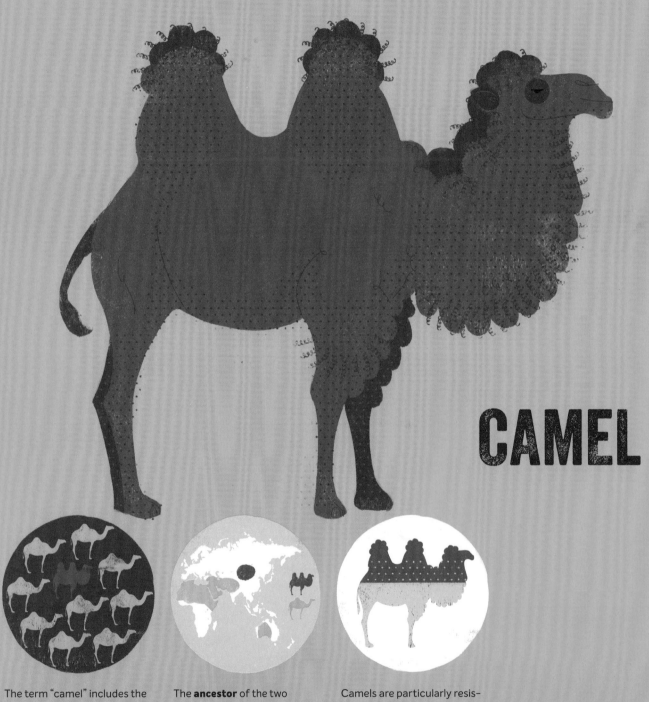

CAMEL

The term "camel" includes the 13 million animals around the world that belong to the genus *Camelus*. Oddly, nine out of ten of them are dromedary camels!

The **ancestor** of the two animals appeared in North America around 40 million years ago. The precursor to the dromedary then spread through the Arabian Peninsula and northern Africa, while the precursor to the Bactrian camel spread to eastern Asia.

Camels are particularly resistant to **dehydration** and can lose up to 30 percent of their body's water. By comparison, humans have difficulty surviving after losing 12 percent.

	CAMEL	DROMEDARY
CLASS	• Mammalia	• Mammalia
DISTRIBUTION	• Mongolia, Turkey, Iran, and China, among others	• From the Western Sahara to India, as well as Australia
HABITAT	• Arid and semiarid environments	• Arid and semiarid environments
DIET	• Dried leaves, thorny vegetation, and seeds	• Dry grasses, thorny plants, and almost anything that grows in the desert
SIZE	• Approximately 10 feet (3 metres) long	• Approximately 10 feet (3 metres) long
WEIGHT	• 992 to 2,200 pounds (450 to 1,000 kilograms)	• 882 to 1,300 pounds (400 to 600 kilograms)
DISTINGUISHING FEATURES	• Two humps	• One hump
LIFESPAN	• 40 years	• 40 years

DROMEDARY

Most Bactrian two-humped camels are **domesticated** and are used for riding or as beasts of burden. Some camels have remained wild in Mongolia, China, and Turkey.

If you cross a Bactrian camel with a dromedary, you get a **dromel**, which has just one hump sometimes with a slight division in the middle.

Camel racing is a very popular activity in Dubai and Qatar. Extremely fast, the animal is capable of running 109 yards (100 metres) in 9.8 seconds, almost as fast as Usain Bolt!

Two wild animals, proudly bearing their antlers likes crowns. Sometimes hunted and rarely tamed, reindeer (a type of deer) prefer the cool—and even the cold— over hot regions.

DEER

The branched **antlers** of male deer and reindeer fall off each year at the end of winter before growing back. In reindeer, both the male and female have antlers; the female's fall off after giving birth, then grow back again.

Deer are usually brown (though sometimes white, in very rare cases!) while reindeer can be brown, gray, and white, or a combination of those colors. Deer and reindeer both typically have a **white rump**.

In the deer family, the female is called a **doe**, the baby is a **fawn**, and the family group is known as a **herd**. When the young males grow up, they are called **stags**.

REINDEER

	DEER	REINDEER
CLASS	• Mammalia	• Mammalia
FAMILY	• Cervidae	• Cervidae
DISTRIBUTION	• Every continent, with the exception of Antarctica and Australia	• Cold regions in the Northern Hemisphere
DIET	• Nuts, fruits, grass, plants, and mushrooms	• Grass in summer; moss, lichen, and mushrooms in late winter
DISTINGUISHING FEATURES	• Males have antlers	• Both males and females have antlers
LIFESPAN	• 4.5 to 15 years	• 15 years (female); 4.5 years (male)

In **Canada**, wild reindeer are called caribou, which happens to be a type of moss that Canadian reindeer love to eat.

In **Lapland**, reindeer are semi-domesticated and used for their milk, meat, and skin, and as a working animal. According to lore, reindeer pull Santa Claus's sleigh.

During mating season, **deer** make noises that often sound like a bellow. The cry that you might hear from the end of August until October allows them to find a mating partner.

Buzzzzz! What's that sound? Equipped with six legs and two pairs of wings each, bees and wasps fly and land, guided by the scent of flowers—or a picnic. They may both be small, but watch out for their stingers!

BEE

Whether wasp or bee, only the female can sting. The **stinger** at the end of her abdomen is connected to glands that produce venom.

While a wasp can sting several times in succession, a bee only has **one try**. As soon as it stings, the bee's abdomen muscles are pulled off along with its stinger, resulting in its death.

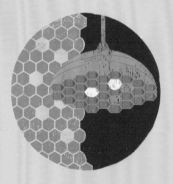
While the **hive** where social bees live is made of wax, a social wasp's **nest** is made of chewed-up wood and other fibers. (Solitary bees and wasps live in holes in the ground.)

	BEE	WASP
CLASS	• Insecta	• Insecta
NUMBER OF SPECIES	• More than 20,000	• Tens of thousands
DIET	• Nectar produced by flowers	• Nectar produced by flowers, insects, and spiders
DISTINGUISHING FEATURES	• Hairiness, lives in a hive (social bees)	• Clear distinction between the abdomen and the body, giving it an "hourglass" figure, lives in a nest (social wasps)
SOCIAL LIFE	• Solitary or social	• Solitary or social
ACTIVITIES OF INTEREST	• Produces wax, honey, and royal jelly • Pollinizes 80 percent of flowering plants	• Hunts insects to feed its larvae • Excellent natural insecticide
LIFESPAN	• Around 122 to 152 days	• Around 12 to 22 days for sterile females and fertile males; 12 months for queens

WASP

If you're stung by a wasp or a bee, **remove the stinger**, then ice the stung area.

To produce **0.04 ounces (1 gram) of honey**, it takes 4,500 flowers. A bee can pollinate 250 flowers per hour.

Insecticide is responsible for the disappearance of bees. But they also suffer from the destruction of their natural habitat: the fewer flowers there are to pollinate, the fewer resources they have to survive.

Completely still, eyes at the water's surface, the crocodile and the alligator watch and wait. Prey approaches. In a flash, they seize it with their tooth-filled snout, dragging it to the bottom of the water to drown it. If you don't know the difference between these two amphibious reptiles, you're not alone: they're often confused with each other.

CROCODILE

When its snout is closed, an alligator's **lower teeth** aren't visible. A crocodile, however, reveals its lower teeth, one of which is lodged in a notch in the upper jaw.

The teeth of crocodiles and alligators regrow when lost! An alligator might go through 3,000 teeth in a lifetime. These reptiles also have a **secondary palate** that resembles a beak, allowing them to open their mouths under water.

A mother crocodile digs her **nest** in the sand. When the eggs hatch, she helps the babies emerge and carries them to the water's edge in her snout.

	CROCODILE	**ALLIGATOR**
CLASS	• Reptilia	• Reptilia
DISTRIBUTION	• Tropical regions around the world	• America, mainly. One species in China.
HABITAT	• Flowing water, lakes, and marshes	• Flowing water, lakes, and marshes
DIET	• Insects, for the young ones; fish, mollusks, and large mammals, for adults	• Fish, frogs, ducks, raccoons, and beavers
SIZE	• Up to 20 feet (6 metres) long for the adult male	• 4 to 13 feet (1.2 to 4 metres) long
DISTINGUISHING FEATURES	• Average snout with a triangular head	• Large snout with a rectangular, flat head
LIFESPAN	• 50 to 75 years	• 50 years in the wild; up to 70 in captivity

ALLIGATOR

The **longest Nile crocodile** was 20 feet (6 metres) from tip to tail—that's as tall as a two-story building!

Crocodiles and alligators have only one cousin, the **gavial**, which can be found in Pakistan, northern India, Nepal, Bhutan, Bangladesh, and Myanmar. Males can be 12 to 15 feet (3.6 to 4.5 metres) long.

The **caiman** belongs to the same family as alligators. There are two species in Central and South America, which measure between 2 feet (0.6 metres) and 4 feet (1.2 metres) long.

Penguins on parade! Wait a minute—
let's take a closer look. Is that an auk?

PENGUIN

MANCHOT

PENGUIN PINGÜINO

It's easy to confuse the English **name** of this bird if you speak French, since penguin is *manchot* in French, and auk is *pingouin*.

Of the **three species of auks**, the little auk, or dovekie (*Plautus alle*), and the razorbill, or razor-billed auk (*Alca torda*), are the only ones still living today. (The great auk was hunted to extinction by the mid-19th century.) There are 18 different species of penguin.

	PENGUIN	AUK
CLASS	• Aves	• Aves
FAMILY	• Spheniscidae	• Alcidae
DISTRIBUTION	• Southern Hemisphere	• Northern Hemisphere
HABITAT	• Diverse environments, including deserts and forests	• Water; nesting on coastal cliffs and ledges
DIET	• Mostly squid, krill, and fish	• Fish
SIZE	• 14 inches to 3.8 feet (35 centimetres to 1.2 metres)	• 8 to 16 inches (20 to 40 centimetres)
WEIGHT	• 2 to 90 pounds (25 to 40 kilograms)	• 1.1 to 1.7 pounds (500 to 750 grams)
DISTINGUISHING FEATURES	• Wings in the form of flippers, incapable of flight but good for swimming	• Wings, capable of flight and swimming
LIFESPAN	• 8 to 30 years	• 10 to 25 years

AUK

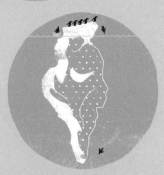

Geography makes the difference! These birds would never be found in the same place: auks live only in the **Northern Hemisphere**, and penguins in the **Southern Hemisphere**.

Emperor penguins are very **resistant to cold**: for them, an ambient temperature of 14° Fahrenheit (–10° Celsius) is equivalent to a temperature of 80° Fahrenheit (27° Celsius) for a naked human.

Penguins routinely dive to a **depth** of 66 to 131 feet (20 to 40 metres), but they can go as deep as 1,312 feet (400 metres)! Their wings, which are really built for swimming, let them reach peak speeds of 22 miles per hour (35 kilometres per hour)!

Auks' **wings** have two functions: in the air, they facilitate flying, while under water they're used for swimming.

With two big ears, tusks and a trunk, the elephant is the largest living animal on land. But depending on whether it lives in Africa or Asia, it can be wild or cohabitate with people.

ASIAN ELEPHANT

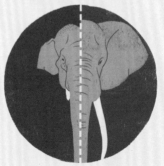

The African elephant is **bigger** than its Asian cousin. It can be up to 13 feet (4 metres) tall and 25 feet (7.5 metres) long and weigh 18,000 pounds (8,000 kilograms). It lives 60 to 70 years on average.

The Asian elephant is **smaller** than the African, and its ears and tusks are also less developed. In a female Asian elephant, the tusks aren't even visible!

In Asia, elephants are often trained and greatly respected, occasionally involved in religious ceremonies. The Hindu god **Ganesha** is represented with an elephant's head.

	ASIAN ELEPHANT	AFRICAN ELEPHANT
CLASS	• Mammalia	• Mammalia
HABITAT	• Humid tropical forests and tropical grasslands	• Deserts, savannas, marshes, river valleys, and forests
DIET	• 112 different plant species and bark	• Grasses, bark, fruit, and roots
DISTINGUISHING FEATURES	• Trunk with one "finger," short tusks, concave and bumpy forehead	• Trunk with two "fingers," long curved tusks, and big ears
LIFESPAN	• 60 to 70 years	• 60 to 70 years

AFRICAN ELEPHANT

The "**fingers**" are the end of the trunk, which is an extension of the nose and upper lip. The African elephant has two fingers, while the Asian elephant has one.

Elephants have **six teeth**, but only use their four molars for chewing. These molars can regrow up to six times. Their tusks correspond to upper incisors.

Due to their **sensitive skin**, elephants look for sources of water to bathe in and cool down. In fact, they don't have sweat glands.

FOOD & DRINK

Whether you find them in a salad or on a pizza, olives infuse food with a Mediterranean flavor. Green or black, sweet or bitter, natural or spiced, you can taste them in many dishes, with or without the pit!

GREEN OLIVE

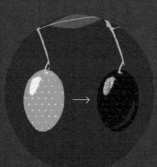

Black olives are picked later than green olives, because olives are **ripe** when the flesh is soft. Green olives are harvested while firm.

The olive **harvest** varies from region to region, generally spanning from October to January, depending on the maturation of the fruits. The color of the olives determines when the harvest begins.

Olives are not good to eat when just picked because they are still too bitter. They must undergo **curing treatments** and special cleaning before ending up in a bowl as an appetizer.

	GREEN OLIVE	**BLACK OLIVE**
TYPE	• Drupe or stone fruit (fleshy fruit with a pit)	• Drupe or stone fruit (fleshy fruit with a pit)
SOURCE	• Olive tree	• Olive tree
HARVEST	• Early (October)	• Late (December to January)
ORIGIN	• Mediterranean basin	• Mediterranean basin
APPEARANCE	• Smooth green skin	• Smooth black skin
NUTRITIONAL BENEFITS	• Vitamin E and fats	• Iron and fats
CALORIC VALUE	• 145 calories per 3.5 ounces (100 grams)	• 167 calories per 3.5 ounces (100 grams)

BLACK OLIVE

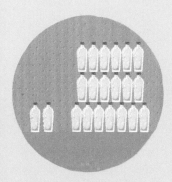

The primary use of olives is to produce **oil**. In the United States, around 2.1 quarts (2 litres) of olive oil are consumed per person, compared with 19 quarts (18 litres) per person in Greece.

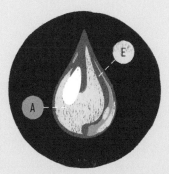

A rich source of **vitamins** and antioxidants, olive oil protects against certain diseases; it has a great reputation when it comes to maintaining good health.

Strawberry or vanilla, in a cup or a cone, one scoop or two—or even three!—these flavored treats are a go-to dessert when it's hot outside. But if you choose raspberry sorbet over raspberry ice cream, are you eating the same thing?

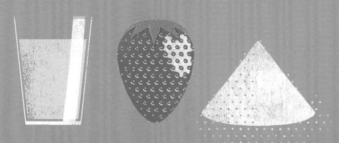

SORBET

A favorite during **antiquity**, sorbets were without a doubt the first of the frozen treats. Served in the court of Alexander the Great in the fourth century B.C., they were icy drinks made of fruit and honey, and the mixture was placed in a container surrounded by snow to freeze the contents.

A precursor to the refrigerator, an **ice box** is a chilled container used to keep food cold. An **ice-cream maker** is a machine that lets you make sorbet and ice cream.

Although we typically enjoy them at dessert, there are also **savory** sorbets—from basil and pepper to avocado and even olive oil!

	SORBET	ICE CREAM
TYPE OF FOOD	• Frozen dessert	• Frozen dairy dessert
ORIGIN	• Far East (China)	• Possibly Italy and France
COMPOSITION	• Water, fruit, and sugar syrup (sometimes egg yolk)	• Milk, cream, and sugar
PRESERVATION	• Between –5° Fahrenheit and 0° Fahrenheit (–20° Celsius and –18° Celsius)	• Between –5° Fahrenheit and 0° Fahrenheit (–20° Celsius and –18° Celsius)
NUTRITIONAL CONTENT	• Possibly some vitamin C	• Calcium
CALORIC VALUE	• Up to 140 calories (one strawberry scoop)	• Up to 140 calories (one chocolate scoop)

ICE CREAM

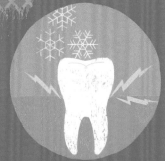

China consumes the most ice cream—more than 1.6 billion gallons (5.9 billion litres) in a year.

Parfaits, profiteroles, and peach Melba are all examples of **frozen desserts**. Peach Melba was created in 1894 by the French chef Auguste Escoffier, as an homage to the Australian opera singer Nellie Melba.

Sometimes, eating ice cream can cause **tooth** pain, a hypersensitivity that warrants choosing a soft toothbrush and sometimes eliminating acidic food.

Chocolate comes in countless forms—baked into brownies, squished inside gooey s'mores, frothed in a mocha, and shaped into popular candy bars. And let's not forget rich hot chocolate topped with whipped cream! But pay attention to the color: Depending on whether it's dark or white, chocolate has a different taste.

WHITE CHOCOLATE

Grown in pods, **cocoa beans** are fruit of the cocoa tree. This small tree of 16 to 26 feet (6 to 12 metres) in height originates from South and Central America.

White chocolate was first marketed by the company Nestlé in Switzerland in the 1930s.

	WHITE CHOCOLATE	**DARK CHOCOLATE**
SOURCE	• Cocoa butter	• Cocoa beans
ORIGIN	• Popularized by Nestlé in Switzerland	• Central and South America
FORM	• Liquid, powder, or bar	• Liquid, powder, or bar
DISTINGUISHING FEATURES	• Very sweet	• Sweet or bitter
COMPOSITION	• Sugar, cocoa butter, vanilla, lecithin, and powdered milk	• Cocoa liquor, sugar and/or cocoa butter
COCOA CONTENT	• 0 percent	• Minimum 10 percent
NUTRITIONAL CONTENT	• Fats, protein, and some calcium	• Iron, phosphorus potassium, copper, and manganese

DARK CHOCOLATE

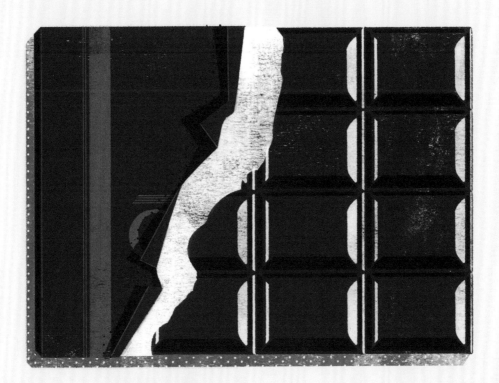

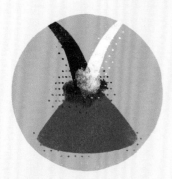

Milk chocolate was invented by Daniel Peter in Switzerland. In 1876, he decided to mix powdered milk with dark chocolate to soften its bitter taste.

While we like to eat chocolate, the **Mayans** used cocoa beans as currency!

What's round, orange, and tangy on the inside? Clementines—and mandarins! Unpeel each one, and you'll find ten or so juicy, sweet segments that you can enjoy as is!

CLEMENTINE

Mandarins have been cultivated in the Far East for about 3,000 years. Some say that they owe their name to the color of the robes worn by **Mandarins**, the high officers of the Chinese Emperor.

A French missionary named Marie-Clement Rodier grew the first **clementines** in Algeria at the end of the 19th century. This small and seedless varietal is a cross between the mandarin and the sweet orange (although some people consider the clementine to be a type of mandarin).

Clementines and mandarins are **winter fruit**. You can eat them from the end of autumn until April.

	CLEMENTINE	MANDARIN
TYPE	• Berry	• Berry
FAMILY	• Rutaceae	• Rutaceae
SOURCE	• Clementine tree	• Mandarin tree
ORIGIN	• Algeria	• Southeast Asia, exported since the 19th century
NUTRITIONAL CONTENT	• Carbohydrates, vitamin C, and vitamin A	• Carbohydrates, vitamin C, and vitamin A
DISTINGUISHING FEATURES	• No seeds, very juicy	• Thin peel

MANDARIN

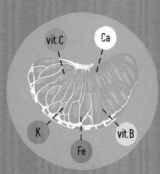

The clementine tree is typically not grown from seed. To produce new fruits, branches are **grafted** onto the trunk of another tree.

Clementines are one of France's favorite fruits, with more than 8.8 pounds (4 kilograms) consumed per person each year. The majority of their clementines are produced in **Corsica**.

Both fruits are known as good sources of **vitamin C**, but they also contain calcium, potassium, iron, and vitamin B6, which are all excellent for your health!

They taste like summer, with skin that's white, yellow, or even deep orange. And they are as delicious eaten alone as in a fruit salad. Whether peach or nectarine, you'll find a pit in the center that is sculpted like a work of art.

PEACH

You can't always trust the **color** of a peach's skin to tell you if it's ripe. There are different varieties, ranging in hue from pink and pale yellow to creamy white and deep red.

Peaches and nectarines are the **same species**, even though they differ slightly in appearance. Peaches feature a soft, fuzzy skin on the outside, whereas nectarines are a genetic variant of the peach—thanks to a recessive allele, they feature smooth, shiny skin instead.

	PEACH	**NECTARINE**
TYPE	• Drupe (fleshy fruit with a pit)	• Drupe (fleshy fruit with a pit)
SOURCE	• Peach tree	• Nectarine tree
HARVEST	• Approximately May through August	• Approximately May through August
ORIGIN	• Likely China	• Recessive gene of the peach
APPEARANCE	• Fuzzy skin	• Smooth, shiny skin
NUTRITIONAL CONTENT	• Vitamin C, antioxidants, fiber, and minerals	• Vitamins A and C and potassium

NECTARINE

In some peach and nectarine varietals (called **clingstones**), the flesh sticks to the pit, while in others (called **freestones**), it doesn't.

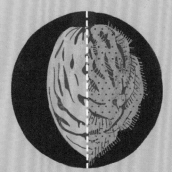

The three largest **peach-producing states** in the United States are California, South Carolina, and Georgia (which is known as the Peach State for peach production dating back to the 16th century, and where the peach is the official state fruit).

While the Latin name for the peach is ***Prunus persica***, it has nothing to do with prunes and doesn't come from Persia: it was first cultivated 7,500 years ago in China.

China is the world's largest producer of peaches and nectarines, at over 10 million tons (9 billion kilograms) per year.

Yes, crustaceans belong on a seafood platter. But while a piece of seafood can certainly be a crustacean, not all seafood belongs to the crustacean family. And, similarly, not all crustaceans are seafood!

SEAFOOD

Seafood includes crustaceans, shellfish, and other small, edible marine animals: like mollusks (such as octopuses, cuttlefish, and snails) and sea urchins.

Crustaceans are **invertebrates** (instead of a backbone, they have an exoskeleton) that most often live in aquatic habitats. However, some have settled on land, like the woodlouse and certain hermit crabs.

Among crustaceans, you'll find those that can **swim** and those that **attach themselves** permanently to a solid base.

	SEAFOOD	CRUSTACEANS
HABITAT	• Marine	• Aquatic, sometimes on land
SIZE	• Varies	• 0.04 inches to 12.5 feet (1 millimetre to 3.8 metres)
DISTINGUISHING FEATURES	• Includes crustaceans and other marine animals	• Two pairs of antennae, often with a shell
NUTRITIONAL CONTENT	• Iodine and vitamin B12	• Vitamin B12
CONSUMPTION	• Edible	• Sometimes edible, sometimes not

CRUSTACEANS

Here are several examples of crustaceans that you might find on a **seafood platter**: lobster, crab, prawn, and shrimp.

The **mussel** is seafood but not a crustacean, because it is a mollusk. The **crayfish** is a crustacean but not seafood, because it evolved in fresh water.

Some **45,000 species of crustaceans** have been identified. The smallest are less than 0.04 inches (1 millimetre), while the largest (like the Japanese spider crab) can be up to 12 feet (3.8 metres) long.

On the plate (and in our minds) noodles can get tangled. In common parlance, eating noodles means the same thing as eating pasta. But at a restaurant, you won't want to confuse noodles with their cousins—shells, tagliatelle, and rigatoni.

NOODLES

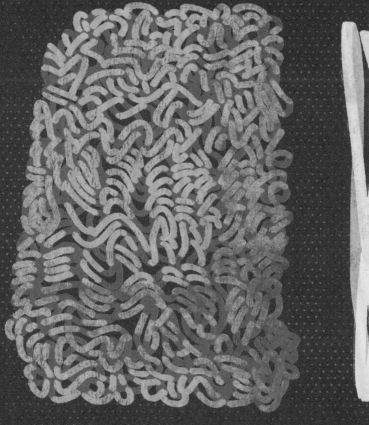

According to legend, the Venetian merchant-explorer **Marco Polo** brought back noodles to Italy in 1295 from his voyage to China.

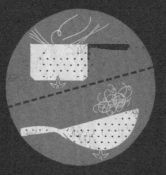

Technically, the **al dente** method of cooking doesn't allow pasta to cook thoroughly, but it's often how connoisseurs like it: firm and crunchy.

Making fresh pasta at home requires a **pasta maker**, which flattens the dough between two rotating cylinders.

PASTA

	NOODLES	PASTA
FOOD CATEGORY	• Starch	• Starch
ORIGIN	• Asia	• Italy
DISTINGUISHING FEATURES	• Thin ribbons	• Many shape varieties including tubes, sheets, and spirals; found fresh or dried
COMPOSITION	• Flour, water, and eggs	• Flour and water (or eggs)
METHOD OF EATING	• Chopsticks or fork	• Fork
ETYMOLOGY	• From the German *Nudel*	• From the Italian *pasta*, "dough"

Italians easily out-eat Americans when it comes to pasta—the average Italian eats over 60 pounds (26 kilograms) of pasta per person, per year, compared to the average American, who eats about 20 pounds (8 kilograms) per person.

Pasta comes in countless **shapes**. There are more than 300 different shapes and varieties of dried pasta in Italy alone.

The 19th century's Art Nouveau movement is sometimes referred to as "**noodle**" style in French because of its use of sinuous forms.

Whether spread on bread or applied to a pan, butter resembles its cousin margarine: greasy, and more or less yellow, making the lips of all who eat it shiny . . . but you can't always tell them apart.

BUTTER

Margarine is often made of **vegetable oil**, such as canola or olive. It contains fats that may help reduce cholesterol levels.

To **make butter**, the cream skimmed from milk is beaten in a churn. Then, the fats are separated from the greasy liquid, drained, and squeezed to make a solid slab.

Butter should be kept in the **refrigerator**, inside a special compartment that prevents it from absorbing the odors of other foods, so that it doesn't spoil too quickly.

	BUTTER	MARGARINE
TYPES	• Sweet, lightly salted, or salted	• Sweet or salted
SOURCE	• Cow's milk	• Fat from vegetables plus water and/or milk
INVENTION	• More than 4,500 years ago	• Late 1860s
PRODUCTION	• Natural	• Industrial
NUTRITIONAL CONTENT	• Low levels of vitamins A and D, fat	• Low levels of vitamins A and D, fat
SHELF LIFE	• 4 to 5 weeks	• 2 to 3 months

MARGARINE

The **color** of butter changes depending on the season and the diet of the cow. Butter from spring and summer has a deep golden-yellow color, while butter sold in winter is closer to white.

While margarine **softens** immediately outside of the refrigerator, butter gets hard in the cold and soft in the heat. It's better to remove it from the refrigerator ahead of time so you don't break your crackers while trying to spread it!

In French, if someone has a black eye, you say they have **"an eye of black butter."** That comes from a 19th century recipe in which eggs are poached in butter that's been blackened on the stove.

GEOGRAPHY

Welcome to the mysterious world of caverns! When you venture inside you may behold stalactites and stalagmites, which are the work of water, rock, and time.

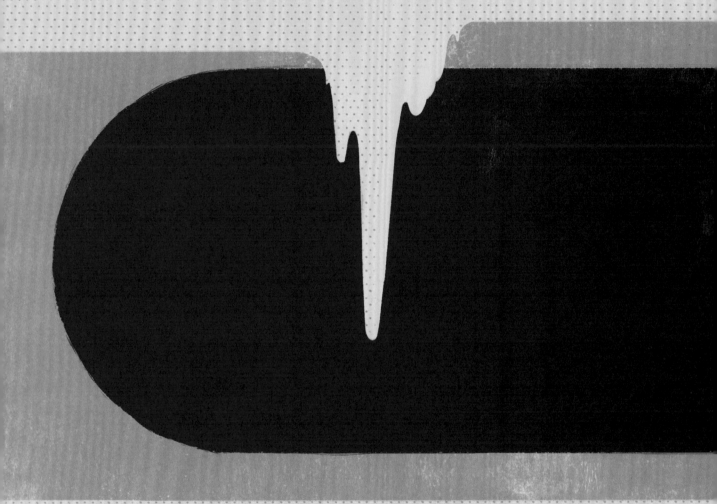

STALACTITE

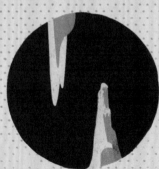

Here's a **mnemonic** to tell stalactites and stalagmites apart: the stalac*tite* has to hold on "tight" to the cavern's ceiling.

Water flows through the rock and enters the cavern saturated in **calcium bicarbonate**. Drop after drop, it deposits the calcium bicarbonate, which crystalizes and accumulates over time into beautiful cavern formations.

	STALACTITE	STALAGMITE
NATURE	• Limestone formation	• Limestone formation
SITE OF FORMATION	• Ceiling	• Floor
FORM	• Long vertical cone	• Long or compact vertical cone
COLOR	• Variety	• Variety
COMPOSITION	• Calcite (calcium carbonate)	• Calcite (calcium carbonate)
ETYMOLOGY	• From the Greek *stalaktos,* "which trickles drop by drop"	• From the Greek *stalagmos,* "flow"

STALAGMITE

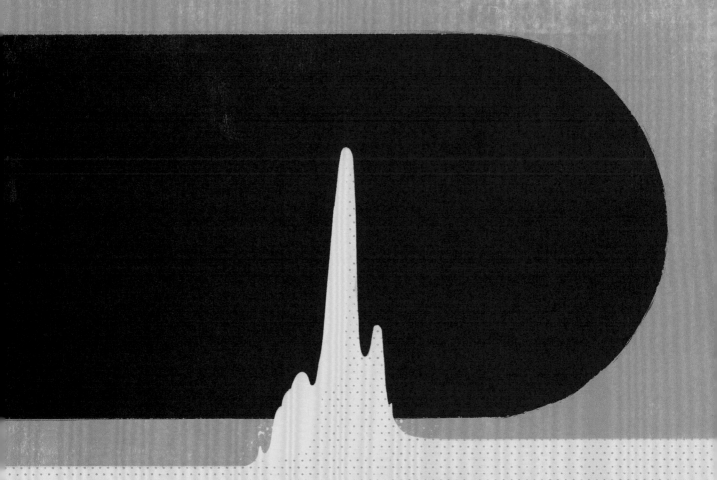

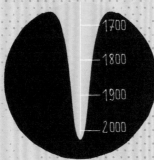

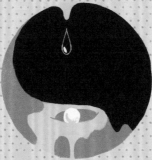

Stalagmites are often positioned underneath stalactites. When the two formations join, they become a **column**.

On average, it takes **100 years** for a stalactite to grow a little over 0.5 inch (1 centimetre). Some say that the longest stalactite in the world is in the Jeita grotto in Lebanon. It is **27 feet (8.2 metres)** tall.

When a stalactite trickles onto a grain of sand, sometimes it will form a **"spherule"** (cave pearl).

When the ceiling of the cavern is sloped, sometimes the water droplets follow the same path and deposit calcium carbonate little by little to form very thin concretions called **draperies**.

If you venture out onto the "high seas," you're actually navigating the ocean. And, while there, if you drink a glass of the water outside your boat, it will be full of salty seawater. So, what is it? Ocean or sea?

SEA

Large, landlocked bodies of water are not seas, technically speaking, even if their water is salty, because a sea must connect to an ocean. So the Caspian Sea and the Dead Sea are actually **salty lakes**.

Together, seas and oceans spread across 71 percent of the Earth's surface. The **Pacific Ocean**, the biggest of them all, covers one-third of the planet.

The **ocean floor** is very uneven, like the surface of the continents: it is punctuated by trenches, canyons, mountain ranges, and even volcanoes.

Panthalassa is the name given to the ancient ocean. Some 250 million years ago, it surrounded Pangaea, a supercontinent that was a block of all the continents merged together.

	SEA	OCEAN
NATURE	• Expanse of saltwater	• Vast expanse of saltwater surrounding the continents
NUMBER	• More than 150	• 5 (Arctic, Atlantic, Southern, Indian, Pacific)
GREATEST SURFACE AREA	• 1.8 million square miles (4.7 million square kilometres) (Arabian Sea)	• 140 million square miles (360 million square kilometres) (71 percent of the Earth's surface)
MARINE CIRCULATION	• Hot and cold currents	• Hot and cold currents

OCEAN

Oceans play an essential role in our **climate**, producing oxygen and absorbing the equivalent of 30 percent of the world's carbon dioxide emissions.

The **maximum depth** reached by humans is 6.8 miles (10.9 kilometres), in the Mariana Trench. The first people to reach that depth were two scientists from the U.S. Navy aboard a submarine in 1960, followed by James Cameron's 2012 dive.

The air is heavy, the wind begins to blow, and the sky darkens. Time to take shelter! Bolts of light streak through the sky, followed by a dull, rumbling sound several seconds later. Lightning and thunder always come together.

LIGHTNING

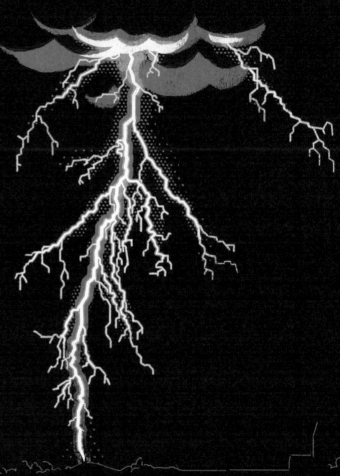

A storm begins in a **cloud**. When the difference in electrical charge becomes too great between the top and the bottom of the cloud, or the bottom of the cloud and the ground, the discharge that causes lightning and thunder brings it back into equilibrium.

Cumulonimbus are the type of clouds that generate lightning. Each cumulonimbus cloud is made of drops of water at its base and crystals of ice at its peak.

	LIGHTNING	THUNDER
NATURE	• Electric discharge	• Sound phenomenon
SOURCE	• Cumulonimbus clouds	• Air heated by lightning
MANIFESTATION	• Bright, wavy line or luminous sheet	• Rumble (far away) or clap (close)
SPEED	• 220,000,000 miles per hour (354,055,680 kilometres per hour)	• 750 miles per hour (1,207 kilometres per hour)
CHARACTERISTICS	• 3 to 5 miles (5 to 8 kilometres) in height and just several inches in diameter; forms a material called fulgurite upon striking sand or rock	• One wave of sound for a short, straight bolt, several waves for a branched bolt

CRACK!

THUNDER

Lightning can appear in three places: between the cloud and the ground, inside the cloud, or from one cloud to another.

Lightning rods are installed to protect people and buildings from lighting strikes. These metallic rods attract lightning and safely channel the electric current.

By counting the number of seconds that separate a lightning bolt from the thunder and then dividing by five, you can estimate the **distance** away, in miles, at which the lightning struck.

As soon as a bolt of lightning strikes sand, a particular mineral is formed: **fulgurite**. Under the heat of the lightning, the grains of sand melt and form glass.

A heavy rain falls and the wind blows violently. A whirlwind stirs in the atmosphere, growing and becoming wild. It picks up everything in its path: branches, entire trees, even houses. When a tornado or a hurricane hits, everyone should take refuge in a small, interior room without windows.

TORNADO

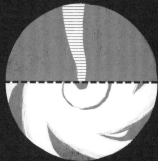

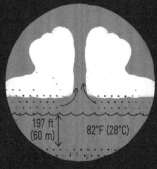

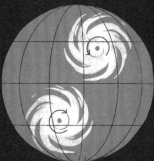

197 ft (60 m) 82°F (28°C)

The **funnel** of a tornado can measure several hundred yards (metres) in diameter. A hurricane funnel can be miles (kilometres).

While a tornado can form over land or over water (the latter is called a **waterspout**), a hurricane needs rotating winds over the ocean, whose water temperature must be a minimum of 82° Fahrenheit (28° Celsius). That's why hurricanes only exist in the tropics.

In the Southern Hemisphere, a **hurricane** is called a cyclone. In the northwest Pacific, it is called a typhoon. In tropical America, it is a cyclone.

In the Northern Hemisphere, the **rotation** a hurricane moves counterclockwise. In the Southern Hemisphere, it moves clockwise.

	TORNADO	HURRICANE
NATURE	• Storm phenomenon	• Atmospheric disturbance
SOURCE	• Thunderstorm	• Ocean
DIMENSIONS	• A few hundred yards (metres) in diameter	• Usually about 300 miles (483 kilometres) wide
FORMATION	• Updrafts from the Earth's surface	• Wind and warm ocean air
MOVEMENT	• Spiral	• Spiral
SPEED OF TRAVEL	• Around 10 to 20 miles per hour (16 to 32 kilometres per hour)	• 10 to 34 miles per hour (16 to 55 kilometres per hour)
WIND SPEED	• Up to 318 miles per hour (512 kilometres per hour)	• A minimum of 74 miles per hour (119 kilometres per hour) on average
DURATION	• From several seconds to several hours	• Up to more than two weeks

HURRICANE

ALBERTO
BERYL
CHRIS
DEBBY
ERNESTO
FLORENCE
GORDON
H...

The center of a hurricane appears black on satellite images, because it has no clouds. This area has relatively calm weather and is called the **eye** of the hurricane.

Each hurricane has its own unique **name**. The first hurricane of the year begins with an A, followed by a B, etc. The names given alternate between male and female.

If the solar system were a playing field, it would be a gigantic stadium. On its expansive surface, small, gleaming marbles of varying sizes would move around. But what do these marbles represent: planets or stars?

STAR

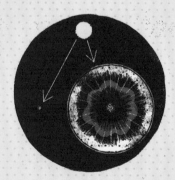

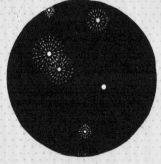

Unlike planets, stars change in size and have a limited lifespan. A star's **death** is brought about in two ways: either it's extinguished after expending all of its reservoirs of gas, or it explodes.

In the sky, you mostly see twinkling stars. But you can also see some planets with **the naked eye**, like Mercury, Venus, Mars, Jupiter, and Saturn, which shine without twinkling.

There are **eight planets** in our solar system: Mercury, Venus, Earth, Mars, Jupiter, Saturn, Uranus, and Neptune. Since 2006, Pluto has been considered a dwarf planet.

	STAR	PLANET
NATURE	• Celestial body	• Celestial body
FORM	• Mostly spherical	• Quasispherical
FORMATION	• Contraction of clouds and gas	• Accretion (condensation and agglomeration of matter)
COMPOSITION	• Gas (hydrogen and helium)	• Gas, ice, or rock
MOVEMENT	• Travels	• Rotates and travels, while orbiting around a star
RADIATION	• Emits light	• Reflects the light of a star

PLANET

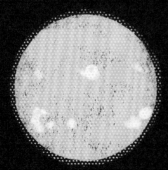

The star we know best is the **sun**. But from the Earth, some 6,000 stars are visible with the naked eye, and there are hundreds of billions of stars in our galaxy.

Venus, the second planet from the sun, is sometimes referred to as "the star of Berger," which translates to "star of the shepherd." Because it is positioned close to the sun, it reflects more light than other planets, and was useful as an early navigation tool.

The moon is a satellite of the Earth. Though it is the most luminous body in our night sky, it doesn't emit any light, but reflects the light of the sun.

It's cold and everything is white: icebergs, ice floes, glaciers . . . even bears blend into the landscape, camouflaged so they can be better hunters! At the Earth's extremities, you'll find Antarctica and the Arctic: two poles so similar and yet so different.

ANTARCTICA

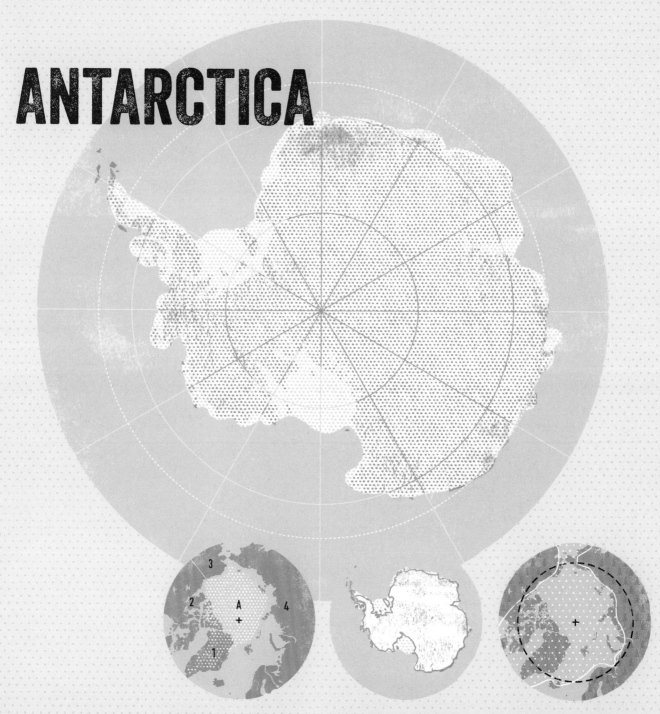

The Arctic includes the Arctic Ocean (A), largely covered in ice floes, and the surrounding landmasses, like Greenland (1), northern Canada (2), Alaska (3), and northern Russia (4).

Antarctica is a continent located over the South Pole. Its surface area is estimated to be 5.5 million square miles (14 million square kilometres). The largest part, covered in ice, is called the **Antarctic ice sheet**.

While the Arctic region doesn't have official **borders**, it roughly corresponds to the zone without trees, inside the Arctic Circle, where the temperature never rises above 50° Fahrenheit (10° Celsius), even in summer.

	ANTARCTICA	THE ARCTIC
NATURE	• Island continent	• Includes oceans, continents, and islands
STATUS	• Governed internationally by the Antarctic Treaty System	• Territory claimed by 5 countries (United States, Russia, Canada, Denmark, and Norway)
GEOGRAPHIC POSITION	• South Pole	• North Pole
SURFACE AREA	• About 5.5 million square miles (14 million square kilometres)	• 7 million square miles (18 million square kilometres)
DISTINGUISHING FEATURES	• Ice formations	• Large reserves of natural gas and oil
BIODIVERSITY	• Little flora, diverse fauna	• Diverse flora and fauna

THE ARCTIC

NORTH STAR

The Arctic takes its name from the constellation **ursa minor** (little bear), in the north. In Greek "bear" is *arktos*. The word *Antarctic* means "opposite the Arctic."

While the **polar bear** is the emblematic animal of the Arctic, the **emperor penguin** lives only in Antarctica. Each year, the **Arctic tern** makes a round trip between the two poles, a distance of around 43,496 miles (70,000 kilometres).

Among the populations living in the Arctic, you'll find the **Inuit people**, who live mostly in Siberia, Alaska, Canada, and Greenland.

It's the birthplace of Gouda, and France calls it "the other country of cheese." It is also known for its famous flower market and the Dutch language. But are we referring to Holland or the Netherlands?

AMSTERDAM

THE NETHERLANDS

0
30 mi
(50 km)

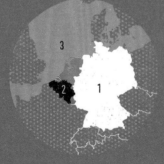

Holland refers to the western part of the Netherlands. It is divided into two provinces: Northern Holland and Southern Holland.

The Netherlands is a member of the **European Union**. Bordered by Germany (1) and Belgium (2), it has the North Sea as a northern border.

The flag of the Netherlands has red, white, and blue stripes. The red stripe used to be orange, the color of the royal family Orange-Nassau. Orange is still the symbolic color of the country.

	NETHERLANDS	HOLLAND
STATUS	• Country	• Provinces of the Netherlands
GOVERNMENT	• Parliamentary democracy	• Each province has a regional government
GEOGRAPHIC POSITION	• Northwestern Europe	• Northwestern Europe
SURFACE AREA	• 16,034 square miles (41,527 square kilometres)	• 2,686 square miles (6,956 square kilometres)
POPULATION	• 17 million	• 6.1 million
LANGUAGE	• Dutch	• Dutch

HAARLEM

THE HAGUE

0 ——— 30 mi
(50 km)

HOLLAND

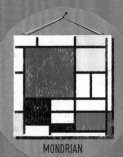

MONDRIAN

The Netherlands, which means the "**lowlands**," is well named: almost a quarter of the land is below sea level. Its numerous canals and dikes help limit the risk of flooding.

Among the **symbols** that represent the Netherlands are windmills, wooden clogs, tulips, Edam cheese, and big soccer clubs like Ajax and PSV Eindhoven.

The 17th century, **the golden age** of Holland, gave rise to master painters like Rembrandt and Vermeer. Other major artists like Van Gogh and Mondrian emerged in the 20th century.

If you cross the English Channel from France, do you end up in England or Great Britain? In both cases, English is spoken, the queen is named Elizabeth II, the pound sterling is the currency, the Beatles are a point of pride, and the flag of the United Kingdom is displayed.

GREAT BRITAIN

30 mi
0 (50 km)

Great Britain includes three entities: England, Wales, and Scotland.

In 1801, the union of Great Britain and Ireland gave rise to the **United Kingdom**. When southern Ireland became independent in 1922, the United Kingdom became known as the United Kingdom of Great Britain and Northern Ireland.

The Union Jack, the British flag, combines the red cross of the English flag, the white X on a blue background of the Scottish flag, and the red X of the Irish flag.

	GREAT BRITAIN	ENGLAND
STATUS	• England, Wales, and Scotland	• Part of Great Britain
GOVERNMENT	• Constitutional monarchy and a parliamentary democracy	• Not an official government or political entity
SURFACE AREA	• 80,823 square miles (209,330 square kilometres)	• 50,301 square miles (130,279 square kilometres)
POPULATION	• 61 million	• 53 million
LANGUAGE	• English (official language), Scots, Ulster Scots, Scottish Gaelic, Irish, and Welsh	• English

ENGLAND

LONDON

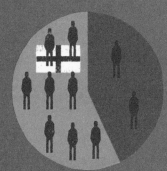

England covers 57 percent of the land in Great Britain, but 86 percent of the population lives there.

While **Elizabeth II** is the head of the United Kingdom, she is also the queen of Canada, Australia, and New Zealand. Fifteen countries of the Commonwealth pledge allegiance to her.

Each of the four nations of the United Kingdom has a **plant** as its symbol: the rose for England, the thistle for Scotland, the leek in Wales, and the clover in Ireland.

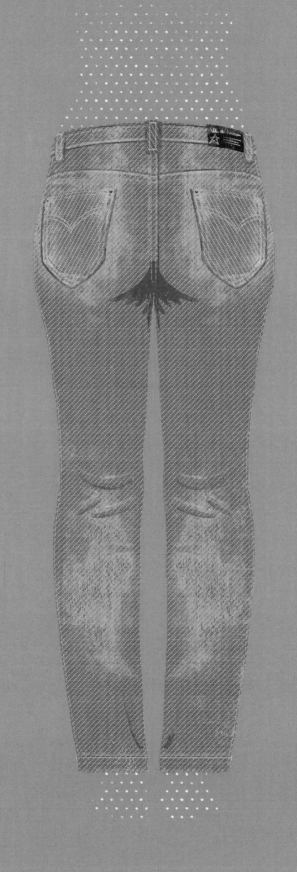

FASHION

SHORTS

As the weather gets warmer, clothing gets lighter and shorter. You swap boots for sandals, a blouse for a tank top, and pants for Bermuda shorts. It's shorts and flip-flops in a heat wave!

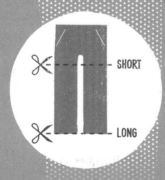

The name **shorts** comes from its definition: a *short* pair of pants worn while playing certain sports or during the summer.

Bermuda shorts get their name from the island of **Bermuda**, where, in the 19th century, British soldiers were required to shorten their pants to stay cool.

BERMUDA SHORTS

	SHORTS	BERMUDA SHORTS
CATEGORY	• Clothing	• Clothing
CUT	• Very short to knee length	• 1 to 3 inches (2.5 to 7.6 centimetres) above the knee
AREA COVERED	• Thigh	• Thigh
MAXIMUM LENGTH	• 1 inch (2.5 centimetres) above the knee	• 1 inch (2.5 centimetres) above the knee
SEASON	• Spring and summer	• Spring and summer

Bermuda shorts hug the thigh and stop just above the knees. Worn with a jacket, shoes, and a tie, Bermudas can also be dressed up.

Playing **sports** sometimes means wearing shorts. That's the case in soccer or in track, where shorts, a tank top, and sneakers are often the only uniform you need.

The tennis tournament **Wimbledon** requires that its participants wear white. In tennis, men generally wear shorts, and women wear a skirt or a dress.

Boy shorts are underwear: very short shorts that sit low on the hips.

TIGHTS

They're opaque, fishnet, or skin-colored, perfect for dressing up or everyday wear. A very thin, sheer fabric lets legs be both clothed and exposed. Stockings and tights are both a close fit, but how do you tell them apart?

Stockings and tights are typically made of **nylon**, a polyamide material that is at once fine, sturdy, and elastic.

To keep them in place, stockings are sometimes attached to a **garter**, a sort of belt that is worn at the waist, rests on the thighs, and hooks onto the stockings.

STOCKINGS

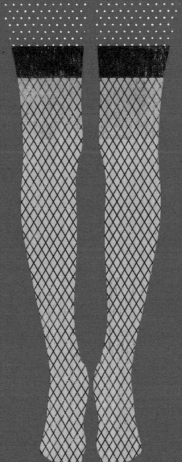

	TIGHTS	STOCKINGS
CATEGORY	• Undergarment	• Undergarment
AREA OF COVERAGE	• From feet to hips	• From feet to thighs
GENDER	• Unisex	• Mostly female
WHEN TO WEAR	• All year	• All year
ELASTICITY	• Flexible	• Flexible

While tights are traditionally associated with women, there are also versions available for **men**, often worn as undergarments in cold regions.

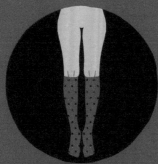

In the family of stockings, there are also **knee-highs**, which stop just below the knee.

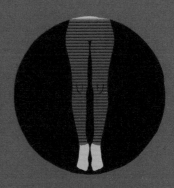

While tights begin like underpants and cover the body from the buttocks to the feet, **leggings** do the same but stop at the ankle.

In the **Middle Ages**, pantaloons were popular clothing for legs. The clothing worn underneath them, from the knee to the foot, later became stockings.

Faded, slim, low rider, boot cut: jeans need their own dictionary to cover the many different cuts and colors! To be precise, the canvas material of blue jeans is called denim, not jean. And, yes—there's a story here . . .

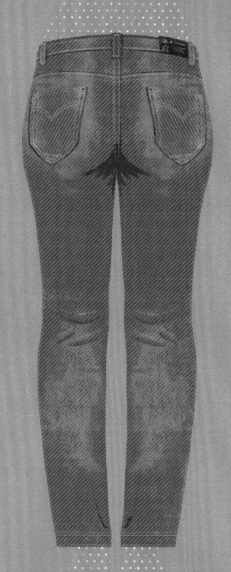

JEANS

The true blue jean originated on May 20, 1873. On that day, **Levi Strauss** received a patent for his pants that were reinforced with rivets and made of blue denim material.

Some say that denim gets its name from the city of **Nimes in France**, where the textile was first created. It refers to a sturdy material made from two threads (blue and white) crossing each other diagonally.

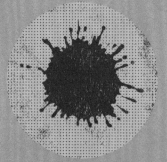

The name *jean* is a reference to the **Italian city of Genoa**, where cotton corduroy (called "jeane" or jean) was manufactured in the 16th century.

	JEANS	DENIM
CATEGORY	• Clothing	• Clothing
TYPE	• Pants	• Textile
ORIGIN	• United States	• France
COLOR	• Blue, white, black, or any color	• Blue (or any color)
COMPOSITION	• Denim or dungaree cloth	• Blue warp thread on unbleached weft
CHARACTERISTICS	• Rivets and topstitched seams	• Durable

DENIM

Black, white, gray, or colored, jeans aren't necessarily made from **blue** denim. And blue denim extends beyond jeans, also used to make skirts, shirts, shorts, jackets, and overalls.

The ancestor of the jean was made from the **canvas of tents**. It was cheap, sturdy clothing intended for mine workers.

Jeans quickly rose to popularity in the 1950s after being stylishly worn by **American movie stars** and then rock 'n' roll icons.

When you're wearing a scarf, gloves, and jacket, it's safe to say that winter has arrived. But when it comes to keeping your head warm, how do you choose between a knit cap and a balaclava?

KNIT CAP

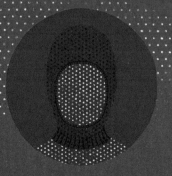

The **knit cap**, soft and without harsh edges, fits tightly. The Medieval Latin precursor was an *abonnis*, which consisted of a band worn around the head. Knit caps can also have ear-flaps, like those worn in Peru.

The **balaclava** does double duty as both a hat, covering the head, and a scarf, covering the neck. Certain models also cover the mouth and nose.

The balaclava can also be made from a hood with holes cut for eyes, called a **ski mask**, and is sometimes associated with bandits hoping to remain incognito.

	KNIT CAP	BALACLAVA
CATEGORY	• Clothing	• Clothing
TYPE	• Headwear	• Headwear
COVERED AREA	• Head	• Head and neck
GENDER	• Unisex	• Unisex
OF INTEREST	• Accessory; protects against the cold	• Mountain equipment; originally worn by soldiers
WHEN TO WEAR	• Winter	• Very cold temperatures

BALACLAVA

While the knit cap can be light and worn to bed as a **nightcap**, the balaclava is only for keeping warm. It is generally knit or made of fleece.

The **Phrygian cap** refers to a conical knit cap worn by freed slaves in ancient Rome. In 1789, it was a symbol of unity with the French Revolution, worn by Marianne, the symbol of the Republic.

At a swimming pool, swimmers must often wear a **swimming cap**. Made of silicone or latex, swimming caps protect hair from chlorine and prevent stray hairs from ending up in the pool.

Some say that the duel between the Stetson and the Borsalino (also known as the fedora) is a match between the United States and Italy: Western cool on the one hand, and Italian flair on the other. In both cases, these head-turning hats harken back to a 1930s style.

STETSON

In 1857, the Italian hatmaker **Giuseppe Borsalino** opened his first boutique. Eight years later, on the other side of the Atlantic, **John B. Stetson** made his mark. They are the fathers of these two legendary hats.

Originally made from **felt**, Stetsons are now also made of straw.

The original Borsalino fedora was characterized by its **2.6-inch (6.5-centimetre) brim**. The hat was made of felt, from the hair of rabbits or hares.

	STETSON	BORSALINO
CATEGORY	• Headwear	• Headwear
TYPE	• Hat	• Hat
MATERIAL	• Felt or straw	• Felt
ORIGIN	• United States	• Italy
GENDER	• Unisex	• Unisex
OF INTEREST	• Waterproof, protects against the sun	• Waterproof, keeps its shape

BORSALINO

The Stetson was almost immediately adopted as the emblematic hat of the American West. In fact, it was worn by historical figures like **Buffalo Bill** and **Calamity Jane**.

One of the most high-end Borsalino hats requires **seven weeks** of work and 50 stages of production to make. It has an alligator-skin band and a gold pin.

Today, the Stetson and Borsalino companies also make other types of hats, like the **Panama**, which actually originated in Ecuador, despite its name.

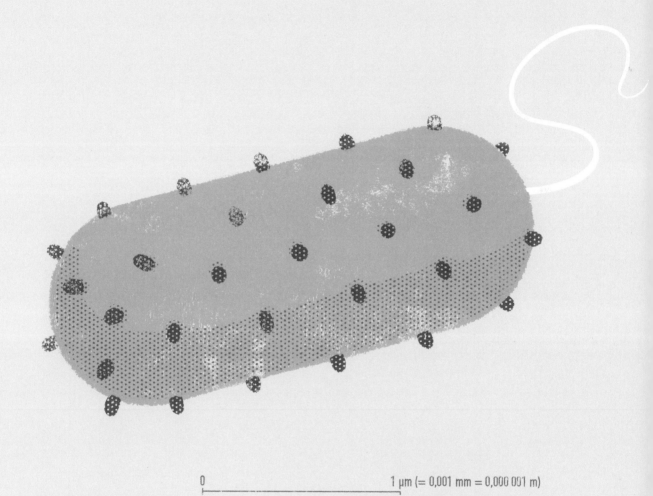

0 ┣━━━━━━━━━━━━━━━━━━━━━━ 1 μm (= 0,001 mm = 0,000 001 m)

HUMAN BODY

In a few months, it will be able to breathe, see, and discover the face of its mother. For now, it knows her from the inside, curled up in her womb, where it will spend nine months developing. But is it a fetus or an embryo?

	EMBRYO	FETUS
NATURE	• Vertebrates and inverte-brates, plants	• An unborn living vertebrate being
PLACE OF DEVELOPMENT	• Uterus, seed, or egg	• Uterus
SOURCE OF FOOD	• Maternal organism or its own nutritional reserves	• Maternal organism
PERIOD	• In humans, up until the end of the 7th week	• From the start of the 8th week until birth for humans
FIELD	• Obstetric gynecology	• Obstetric gynecology

EMBRYO

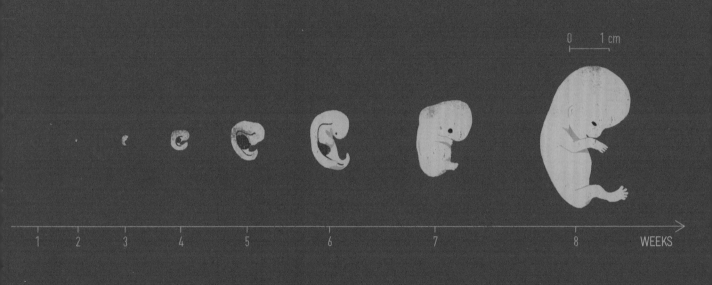

0   1 cm

1   2   3   4   5   6   7   8   WEEKS

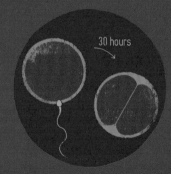

30 hours

In humans, **fertilization** creates an egg cell from the fusion between the nuclei of the egg and sperm. Thirty hours later, this cell divides in two: this is now called an embryo.

An embryo becomes a fetus when all of the **organs have been formed**, and all that is left is to concentrate on the growth and development of the future baby.

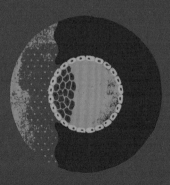

In a medically assisted pregnancy (in-vitro fertilization), an egg is fertilized by a sperm in the lab. The embryo is intro-duced into the uterus between the third and sixth day of life, to implant on the **uterine wall**.

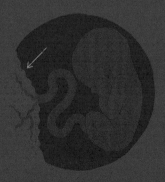

Created over the course of the pregnancy, and functional from three months onward, the **placenta** helps the fetus develop. Toward the end of human pregnancy, it resem-bles a disc around 8 inches (20 centimetres) in diameter and weighs about 1.1 pounds (500 grams).

FETUS

A fetus gets its food from maternal blood. Through the **umbilical cord**, it takes in nutrients and oxygen and expels carbon dioxide and waste.

A fetus's **senses** improve over time: taste and touch are developed at four months. At six months, it can hear sounds from outside the womb.

24 WEEKS

0   1 cm

Two eyes to see the world: they may be brown, blue, or green, sometimes tinted yellow or gray. In the center of that color is a round, black well. Iris and pupil, the two make a pair.

IRIS

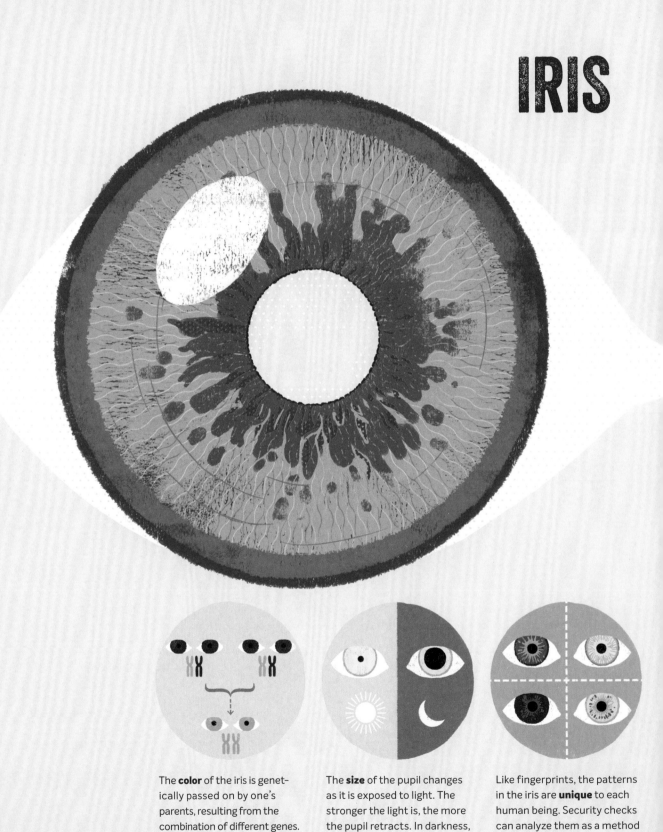

The **color** of the iris is genetically passed on by one's parents, resulting from the combination of different genes.

The **size** of the pupil changes as it is exposed to light. The stronger the light is, the more the pupil retracts. In darkness, the pupil dilates.

Like fingerprints, the patterns in the iris are **unique** to each human being. Security checks can analyze them as a method of identification.

	IRIS	PUPIL
NATURE	• Pigmented muscular curtain	• Central opening of the iris
POSITION	• Vertical	• Vertical
APPEARANCE	• Striated disc, pierced in the center	• Round
COLOR	• Varies	• Black
ACTION	• Contraction, dilation	• Contraction, dilation
FUNCTION	• Regulates the size of the pupil	• Regulates the entry of light into the eye

PUPIL

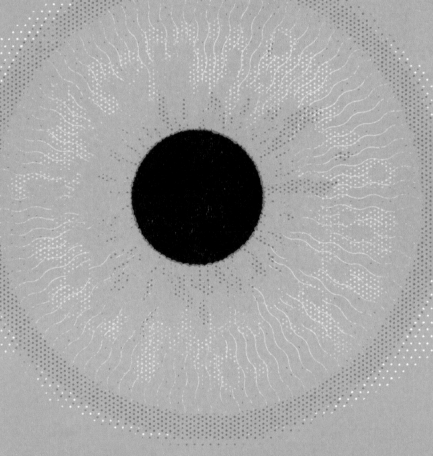

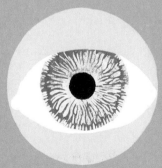

In people with **albinism**, the iris has no pigment and is often described as having red undertones. Albinism causes sensitivity to light.

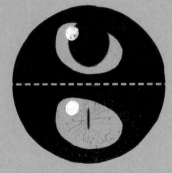

In animals with very good **night vision**, like cats or owls, pupils can dilate to be very large. During the day, they reduce to a slit.

When a person has irises of two different colors, their eyes are said to have **heterochromia**.

From afar, everything is clear—from the words on signs to the face of someone across the street. But when it comes to looking at a map up close, everything becomes muddled and blurry. Is it presbyopia or farsightedness?

FARSIGHTEDNESS

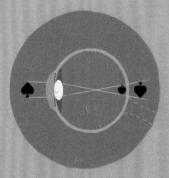

To be clear, an **image** must form on the retina at the back of the eye. In the case of farsightedness, the eye is too short, and the image forms behind the retina. Close objects appear blurry.

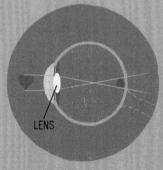

LENS

"Presbyopia" comes from the Greek *presbutes*, which means **"old."** It is caused when the eye's lens—situated behind the iris—becomes inflexible as a result of aging and can no longer adjust one's vision.

Farsightedness frequently occurs in **children**. When the eye grows, the fault in vision corrects itself. Until then, glasses can solve the problem.

	FARSIGHTEDNESS	PRESBYOPIA
NATURE	• Visual anomaly	• Visual anomaly
CAUSE	• The image of an observed object forms behind the retina	• Inability of the lens to properly adjust
ORIGIN	• Physiological or genetic	• Old age
AFFECTED GROUPS	• Children and adults	• Adults over 40
SYMPTOMS	• Difficulty seeing from up close, able to see from afar	• Difficulty seeing from up close
RESULTING ISSUES	• Headache, fatigue, eye redness, squinting	• Need to increase distance of objects to see (12 to 16 inches, or 30 to 40 centimetres)
CORRECTION	• Spontaneous or artificial (wearing corrective lenses, surgery)	• Artificial (wearing corrective lenses, surgery)

PRESBYOPIA

In contrast to farsightedness, presbyopia never spontaneously fixes itself. Little by little, the presbyopic person can no longer go without **glasses** to read.

Among other faults in vision, nearsightedness, or **myopia**, causes bad vision from afar. It's the opposite of farsightedness: the image forms in front of the retina.

Vision challenges can be treated by wearing corrective **glasses**, **contact lenses**, or sometimes through **surgery**.

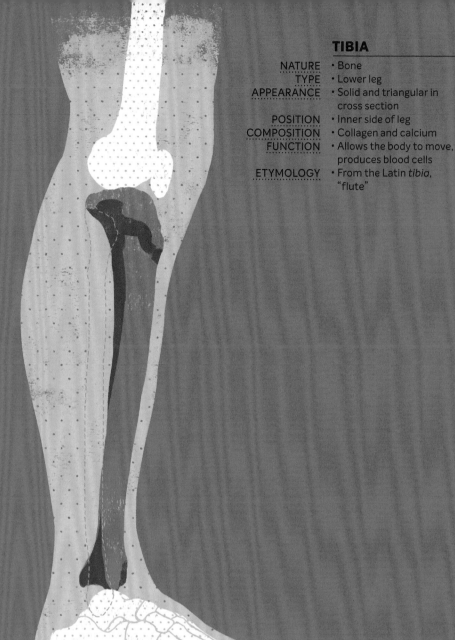

TIBIA

TIBIA

NATURE	• Bone
TYPE	• Lower leg
APPEARANCE	• Solid and triangular in cross section
POSITION	• Inner side of leg
COMPOSITION	• Collagen and calcium
FUNCTION	• Allows the body to move, produces blood cells
ETYMOLOGY	• From the Latin *tibia*, "flute"

They form the structure of our legs. The tibia and the fibula, two long bones connected to each other, help to give our legs their power (along with our muscles). And they sometimes share equally in pain, when a kick or a bad fall causes a fracture to both.

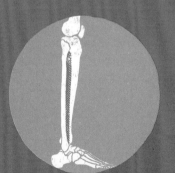

The **interosseous membrane** connects the tibia and fibula. Farther down, the two bones are also connected at the ankle joint.

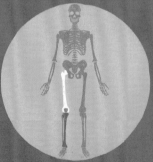

The tibia is one of the largest bones in our skeleton. It supports the weight of the body, which it transfers upward through the **femur** (thigh bone).

FIBULA

- Bone
- Lower leg
- Long and slender

- Outer side of leg
- Collagen and calcium
- Allows the body to move, produces blood cells
- From the Latin *fibula*, "brooch"

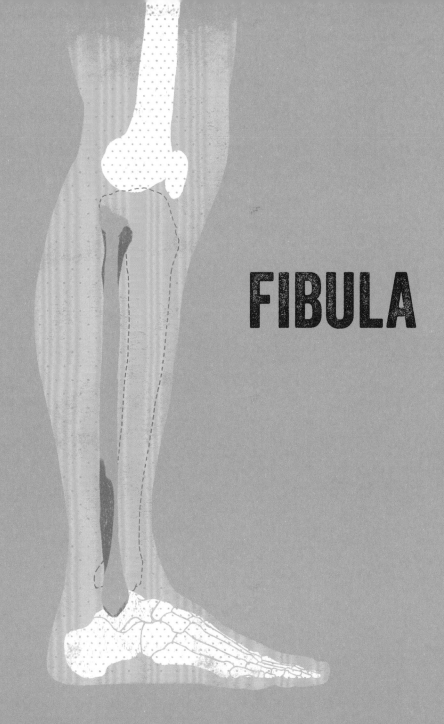

FIBULA

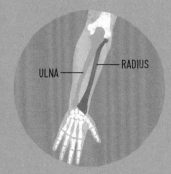

ULNA — — RADIUS

Just like the leg, the **forearm** is made up of two bones connected at their two ends. They are the radius and the ulna.

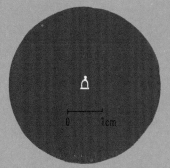

0   1cm

There are **206 bones** in the human body. The smallest bone is the stapes, a bone in the ear. The longest bone is the femur.

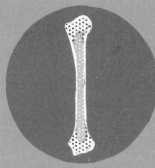

In addition to creating the body's structure, bones also contain **marrow**, which produces red blood cells, white blood cells, and platelets.

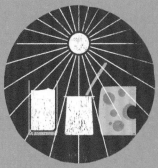

Outdoor activities and dairy products are a recipe for strong bones! When exposed to UV (ultraviolet) rays, the skin synthesizes **vitamin D**, which is essential for absorbing the calcium present in dairy.

A heart beats—it is the breath of life. It's so simple, but an incredible machine is working. Along with the heart, a network of pipes—veins and arteries—transport nutrients to our organs. But what is the difference between these two conduits?

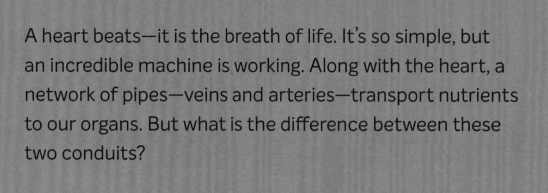

VEIN

Arteries pump blood rich in oxygen, called "red blood," from the heart toward the organs. The main artery in the human body is the aorta.

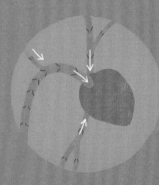

Veins bring blood that is poor in oxygen and full of carbon dioxide, called "blue blood," from the organs toward the heart. The inferior and superior vena cavae are the major veins.

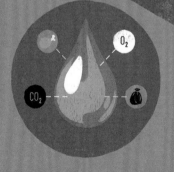

The function of blood is to distribute **oxygen** and essential nutrients to our organs and tissues. It also carries carbon dioxide and other waste from our body to be eliminated.

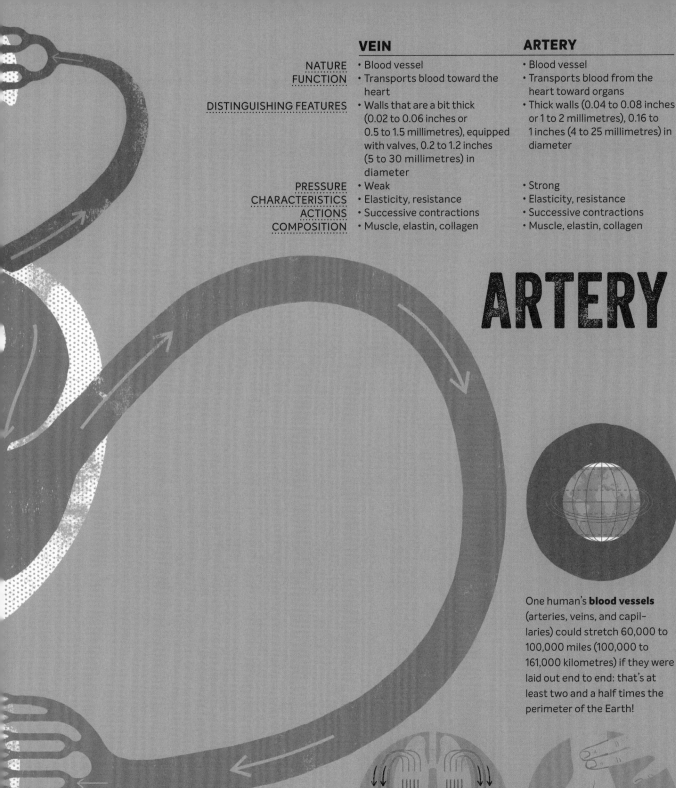

	VEIN	ARTERY
NATURE	• Blood vessel	• Blood vessel
FUNCTION	• Transports blood toward the heart	• Transports blood from the heart toward organs
DISTINGUISHING FEATURES	• Walls that are a bit thick (0.02 to 0.06 inches or 0.5 to 1.5 millimetres), equipped with valves, 0.2 to 1.2 inches (5 to 30 millimetres) in diameter	• Thick walls (0.04 to 0.08 inches or 1 to 2 millimetres), 0.16 to 1 inches (4 to 25 millimetres) in diameter
PRESSURE	• Weak	• Strong
CHARACTERISTICS	• Elasticity, resistance	• Elasticity, resistance
ACTIONS	• Successive contractions	• Successive contractions
COMPOSITION	• Muscle, elastin, collagen	• Muscle, elastin, collagen

ARTERY

One human's **blood vessels** (arteries, veins, and capillaries) could stretch 60,000 to 100,000 miles (100,000 to 161,000 kilometres) if they were laid out end to end: that's at least two and a half times the perimeter of the Earth!

The **lungs** are connected to the heart by an artery so that blood can become oxygenated. Then, four pulmonary veins bring the blood back to the heart, which distributes it.

We use arteries to measure our heartbeat, by taking our **pulse**. To do so, place your fingers on the carotid artery (under the jaw) or on the radial artery (inside of the wrist).

Tuberculosis, leprosy, cholera, not to mention the flu and AIDS: many serious maladies are connected to the presence of organisms (or microbes) in our bodies that are invisible to the naked eye. But is it a virus or bacteria?

BACTERIA

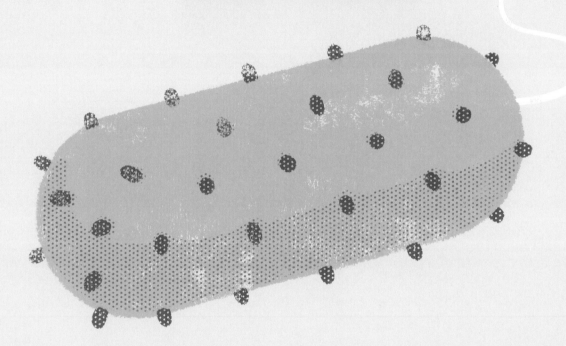

0   1 μm (= 0,001 mm = 0,000 001 m)

Today, we have discovered and documented around **5,000** viruses capable of parasitizing animals and plants.

There are **10,000 species** of bacteria and **30 to 400 trillion bacteria cells** in the human body. That's about as many as our own cells!

While certain bacteria cause disease, most of them play a **beneficial role**. For example, certain bacteria aid in digestion or recycling waste.

	BACTERIA	VIRUS
NATURE	• Unicellular microorganism	• Microorganism
CLASS	• Neither animal nor plant	• Neither animal nor plant
SIZE	• Several micrometers in length	• 10–300 nanometers in diameter
DISTINGUISHING FEATURES	• No nucleus (prokaryote)	• No cell
EFFECT	• Beneficial, in general	• Often infectious
REPRODUCTION	• Cellular division or genetic mixing	• Dependent on host cell
DISCOVERY	• Around 1674	• 1898
ETYMOLOGY	• From the Greek *baktron*, "stick"	• From the Latin *virus*, "poison"

VIRUS

0   1 μm (= 0,001 mm = 0,000 001 m)

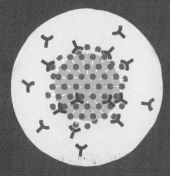

The function of **antibiotics** is to kill or block the multiplication of bacteria. That's why they have no effect if the illness is caused by a virus.

In certain cases, a **vaccine** can prevent an infection and inoculate an organism against the germ. It was due to a major vaccination campaign that the smallpox virus was eradicated in 1980.

Once a virus touches an organism, the organism triggers an **immune response** to defend itself against the next infection.

CITY

or an end-of-year field trip out of the city, a teacher might take their students on a chartered coach. But when traveling to a museum on the other side of town, is a city bus best?

CITY BUS

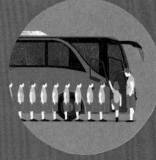

The city bus is a form of **public transportation** in urban areas. Usually, you have to punch your ticket or show a bus pass to the driver in order to ride it.

The chartered coach is a mode of **private transportation**. Generally, a community (like a class or a tourist group) rents this type of vehicle.

A chartered coach and a city bus can also be called a **coach** and a **bus**, respectively. "Mini-coach" and "minibus" refer to vehicles of a smaller size, ideal for serving less frequented areas.

	CITY BUS	CHARTERED COACH
NATURE	• Automotive vehicle	• Automotive vehicle
FUNCTION	• Group transport	• Group transport
LENGTH	• 29 to 40 feet (10.5 to 18 metres)	• Around 45 feet (14 metres)
CAPACITY	• 8 to 100 seats	• 35 to 89 seats
CHARACTERISTICS	• Low floor, seats, and standing places	• High floor, seats, sometimes standing places, compartments for luggage
EQUIPMENT	• Bars and handles, system to request a stop	• Seat belts, tray tables, and toilets
CIRCULATION	• Frequent stops, medium to slow speed	• Infrequent stops, slow to fast speed on the highway (65 miles per hour or 100 kilometres per hour)
COVERAGE	• Urban and semiurban	• From urban to international

CHARTERED COACH

Articulated buses can be more than 60 feet (17 metres) long, weigh 32,000 pounds (14,500 kilograms), and carry 100 passengers.

In London, it's common to see **red double-decker buses**. However, it was in Paris in 1853 that the first double-decker bus was put into circulation.

The **van**, an abbreviation of "caravan," is a type of minibus for transporting people.

Extra, extra! Read all about it! At newsstands, there are publications for all types of people, with subjects ranging from politics to health and international news. Both newspapers and magazines feature a variety of stories, often accompanied by a photo or illustration. But how do you distinguish one from the other?

NEWSPAPER

A newspaper is often a **daily** publication that contains news of all types. They are sometimes called "journals," which is a fitting name, deriving from the Latin *diurnalis* ("of the day").

A magazine is a **periodical** publication, published weekly, monthly, or even bimonthly. It may focus on a particular area of knowledge, like literature or cars.

Newspapers are printed on **newsprint**, a special type of paper.

	NEWSPAPER	MAGAZINE
NATURE	• Periodical publication	• Periodical publication
DOMAIN	• Press	• Press
FREQUENCY	• Daily to quarterly	• Biweekly to quarterly
COST	• Free or paid	• Free or paid
MATERIAL	• Newsprint paper (gray and dull)	• Coated paper (smooth), matte or shiny
ASSEMBLAGE	• Folded	• Stapled or glued
CONTENTS	• Informative (news, announcements) and professional	• Often thematic (news focused on a specific interest)

MAGAZINE

2 JANVIER 2014

NATURE MAGAZINE

ELEPHANT
African or Asian?

"**News**" can refer to any delivery of current events, from print and Web content to radio and television. Many news stories are compiled by global news agencies like the Associated Press (AP), Agence France-Presse (AFP), and Reuters.

"Journal" can also refer to a **notebook** in which events are documented. This can be a personal journal, a logbook, or a travel journal.

Today, the majority of news agencies simultaneously release their content in print and Web form. Subscribers can access Web content in addition to having the physical newspaper delivered or buying it at the store.

In most major European cities, you may glimpse a tower topped by a spire. Bells sound from the belfry, causing pigeons to scatter and soar. But is it a cathedral or a basilica? Both of these monumental landmarks have a storied history, although there is a key difference when it comes to their architectural origins.

BASILICA

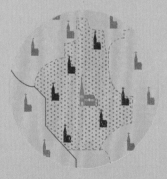

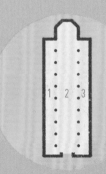

A cathedral is the mother church of a **diocese**, a territorial division of the Catholic Church, with a bishop as its leader. Each diocese has only one cathedral. On the other hand, it can have several basilicas.

Originally, "basilica" referred to a type of **Roman architecture**. It was a large rectangular edifice with three **naves** (the central area of a church). You can find this layout in Christian basilicas.

In ancient Rome, the basilica was a secular place used for civil **gatherings**, rather than religious ones. It served as a place for trials, strolling, and commerce.

	BASILICA	CATHEDRAL
TYPE OF STRUCTURE	• Civil, then Christian, structure; often Catholic	• Christian structure
FUNCTION	• Place of pilgrimage and worship	• Place of pilgrimage and worship
LAYOUT	• Rectangular, then cross-shaped	• Often cross-shaped
CHARACTERISTICS	• Division into major and minor basilicas, insignia (flag and bell chime)	• Luminous, high ceilings, often consecrated
FIRST APPEARANCE	• Second century B.C.	• 12th century
LARGEST IN THE WORLD	• Our Lady of Peace in Yamoussoukro (Ivory Coast)	• St. John the Divine in New York (United States)
ETYMOLOGY	• From the Latin *basileus*, "king, emperor"	• From the Greek *cathedra*, "seat"

CATHEDRAL

In the center of the city of **Saint-Denis** in France, there is a building that is both a basilica and a cathedral. The original church was constructed at the site of the tomb of Saint Denis, the first bishop of Paris.

Cathedrals were the first structures that used the **Gothic style**. They are ornamented with stained glass windows, vaulted arches, and sculptures (for example columns and gargoyles).

Other large, monotheistic religions also have **places of worship**: such as the synagogue for the Jewish religion and the mosque for Islam.

Portals to the outdoors, they offer fresh air and a place of repose. At once connected to an edifice and yet a world unto themselves, the terrace and the balcony are sought for their unique vantage points. Yet what sets them apart?

TERRACE

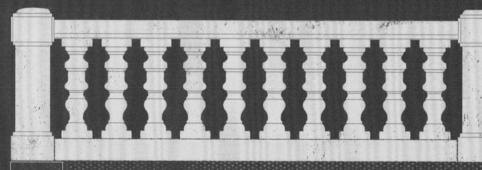

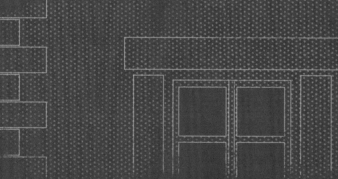

While you can get fresh air on a terrace and on a balcony, the former is located above an **interior room**, while a balcony projects off the side of a building.

When an area is **terraced**, the soil is churned, then flattened. It is then covered with wood, concrete, or flagstone.

In a performance space like a **theater**, the balcony refers to the first gallery of seats above the orchestra.

	TERRACE	BALCONY
NATURE	• Platform on or next to a building	• Platform on a building
TYPES	• Self-supporting, on the ground or on top of a building	• Attached to a building's facade
SITE	• On one level or floor	• A projection of a floor
CHARACTERISTICS	• Slightly elevated	• Floor and ceiling, three closed sides, iron or concrete railings
ETYMOLOGY	• From the Latin *terra,* "earth"	• From the Italian *balcone*

BALCONY

"Terrace" may also refer to an area of the **sidewalk** in front of cafes or restaurants where tables and chairs are arranged to seat customers.

Terraced cultivation refers to a collection of small fields cut into a staircase shape. On each level, bordered by a low stone wall, there is a space for farming. In mountainous regions of Asia, rice is often cultivated this way.

A **loggia** is a sort of balcony that does not project out from a wall. It is connected to the building through a room or gallery.

It's the season of spring cleaning! Time to put away hats and coats to make room for lighter clothing—to empty armoires and closets, only to fill them again. But what is the difference between the two?

CLOSET

An armoire is a piece of furniture that is generally **taller than it is wide**. Behind its doors, the interior space is divided into shelves.

A closet is created in a **niche** or a **recessed wall**. Shelves and clothing racks can be installed to organize clothing.

A closet resembles an armoire, but it is **attached** to the wall, the floor, and the ceiling.

	CLOSET	**ARMOIRE**
CHARACTERISTICS	• Built in, partially built in, or in relief from a wall	• Shelves and suspended bars, panels, with or without drawers
MATERIAL	• Wood, metal	• Wood, metal
POSITION	• Fixed	• Movable, sometimes elevated
FUNCTION	• Organization, storage	• Organization, storage
USAGE	• Home or office	• Typically home

ARMOIRE

Armoire takes its name from the Latin *arma*, which means "tools." An armoire is basically a big cabinet; smaller cabinets include medicine cabinets and bathroom cabinets.

Lower than an armoire, a **dresser** (with drawers) and a **sideboard** (with doors and drawers) are pieces of furniture traditionally used to hold linens and dishes.

INDEX